Beloved

Ginger Usher

Beloved

Copyright © 2014 by Ginger Usher

All rights reserved. No part of this book may be reproduced or transmitted in any form or by any means without written permission of the author.

All Scripture quotations are taken from the King James Version of the Holy Bible (in the public domain.)

ISBN-13: 978-0-9904764-1-2

ISBN-10: 0-9904764-1-3

Printed in the United States of America

RevMedia Publishing
PO BOX 5172
Kingwood, TX 77325

A publishing division of Revelation Ministries

www.revmediapublishing.com

www.gingerusher.com

Cover design by Valerie Hightower

A Word from the Author

If you are presently in the midst of a trying situation, remember this… "This too shall pass" As you read this book, allow yourself to believe and receive every promise.

The Dream

A few years ago, during a very difficult time, I had the most vivid dream; a dream that became the focal point of this book.

I saw the most beautiful crown. It was gold, and covered in precious jewels. It was displayed like a royal treasure. Suddenly, fireworks began exploding behind it. It seemed as if there was a celebration going on.
Then, I heard a voice, saying,
"Will you wear my crown?"

The Song of Songs

1:1: "The Song of Songs, which is Solomon's."

A Jewish Scholar said, "Like Jesus is the King of Kings, The Song of Solomon is the Book of Books."

In prayer, the Holy Spirit spoke to me and said, "Women have closed their wombs. The Song of Solomon will open their wombs."

You must allow the Holy Spirit to reveal His plan. Are you still conceiving His Word, and bringing to birth those things He desires to manifest in the earth? Or are you carrying scar tissue because of wounds you have endured? *Beloved,* only He knows, and no one else needs to. You need to ask yourself, "am I willing to conceive, and endure the process, once again?"

Dedication

Thank you:

To my Beloved Savior and King, Jesus, to the Precious Holy Spirit and to my Heavenly Father, for giving me the divine privilege to write this beautiful book.

To my darling husband Gene for always supporting me and encouraging me. I love you.

To my family Amy, David, Valarie, Clint, Doug, Courtney, Naomi, Morgan, Natalie, Tyler, and Carter. You are truly the heartbeat of my life.

Special thanks to my granddaughter Courtney for hours spent typing and pondering over written words.

Foreword

It is an Honor for me to write this recommendation for Ginger Usher's book.
This book is full of "Golden Nuggets" that will help you to comprehend and glean wisdom from the Song of Solomon.

Ginger was taught these truths by the Holy Spirit and reflects them in her personal relationship to her Earthly husband Gene, others and most of all her Heavenly Father.

As you put this wisdom into practical application your marriage and life will be changed.

Read and Enjoy!

Blessings
Dr. Gary Wood
Author A Place Called Heaven

Table of Contents

Chapter 1 9
Chapter 2 38
Chapter 3 56
Chapter 4 65
Chapter 5 80
Chapter 6 92
Chapter 7 100
Chapter 8 107

Song of Solomon

Chapter 1

1:2: "Let Him kiss me…"

Beloved, this book is not about the world. It's not about the church.

It's about you!

No matter how busy or successful you become, it's all about your relationship. You are not just part of the family, you belong to Him. You are the one called to sit in your place beside Him! You need to be willing to embrace your kingdom responsibilities.

He needs you to reign in your high place, but are you willing?

1:2: "…with the kisses of his mouth…"

It's been said, "Whoever has your ear has your future." Who is the voice in your ear? Who speaks to you? Who are you listening to?
Kisses are expressions of love, and the expressions of His mouth are His words. He alone knows how to cause you to take your royal place in His kingdom. Those living outside the chamber of the King have no knowledge of His protocol.
Will you continue to allow them to hold you back? Or will you throw all caution to the wind and begin, again, to chase Him?

1:2: "…for your love is better than wine."

We are eternally betrothed unto Him who knew and loved you before all existence of what we see. He who breathed life into Adam will also breathe life into you.
It hasn't been too long. The devil is a liar. Your spirit is as young as it ever was. He will touch you. You will live again in the spirit. "Out of your belly will flow rivers of living water," refreshing and reviving you.

1:3: "Because of the savor (fragrance) of thy good (holy) ointment (anointing)."

Nothing triggers our memory like the sense of smell. It brings an instant reminder of an experience.
The Holy Spirit is desiring to bring to your remembrance, those intimate encounters with the one you love.
No one has ever touched you the way He has. Your spirit will remember where you were, and also the depth of passion that was ignited.

1:3: "…Your name is an ointment poured forth…"

Just the mention of the name "Jesus" changes the atmosphere. Just like a pleasant fragrance fills the air, His name will fill your spirit.
Whatever may be in your life that is hindering, change it by speaking His name. As you do, the presence of the Holy Spirit will be poured out for you.

Say His Name!

1:3: "...Therefore do all the virgins love thee."

Your spirit was created to love Him. "As He is, so are you in this world,"-1 John 4:17.

He is Love.

You are never more alive than when you are actively pursuing Him.
Virgins are those who are pure in heart. They know Him and have experienced the depth of his love. No one needs to tell them. They know him intimately. Many hours have been spent in His presence. They know His touch and His love.

1:4: "Draw me..."

You have so much to do. Just like Martha, you are a person of responsibility. That's why you have the position you have. Your love for Him keeps you very busy. After all, He said, "Whatever you find yourself doing, do it with all your might". That's what you are doing. How can you do more? Maybe that's not the question. Could you possibly do less? Can you turn your attention to Him like Mary did?

He said to her, "You have chosen the better thing. What have you chosen? Choose Him today. Choose Him over something that may seem more important.

1:4: "…we will run after thee…"

Nothing else will affect your life and/or ministry like chasing after Him. As you do, those whom your life influences will be touched by the fresh anointing on your life.
Doesn't The Word say in Psalm 133, "The oil runs down"? It will flow onto you and onto them. They will experience the oil of his presence because you chose to run after Him.
What ever you have on your agenda today, put it aside and run after Him.

1:4: "…the King has brought me into His chamber…"

Because He is your priority, He will begin to reign over all that concerns you.
As you lay down your schedule and sit at His feet, He will be King over your present and over your future.
He will speak, and His word will manifest for what you cannot do. He is able. He will decree, and it will

be done. Psalm 103:20 says, "…angels hearken to the voice of His word".

Like Esther, you will be granted access into His chamber. Notice,

He brought you in!

He desires to do for you, what you have been asking for. He will reign over you.

1:4: "…we will be glad and we will rejoice in thee…"

Glory to God!

How wonderful it is to know that you have been granted your hearts desires, and to see others rejoicing in their miracles. Isn't that what this is all about? To help others, and to see them healed, set free, and prospering. Could it be? Could it possibly be that you have neglected the very source of life needed? Ask the Holy Spirit to reveal to you this truth. Be honest with yourself. Are you being all He desires you to be? Or are you laboring?

1:4: "…we will remember thy love…"

What changed you? His love! What will change others? Only His love! They need Him. They need His touch. The oil accumulated in your spirit will overflow unto them.
Remember how His touch healed your spirit, your soul and your body? He is able to embrace and supply all their needs. You cannot fix them. You cannot fix yourself. Your beautiful programs, and generous gifts, cannot replace time spent in His presence.
Just one touch from Him heals, restores, and changes. Remember who healed you? It wasn't the church.

It was Him!

1:4: "…we will remember your love, more than wine…"

Wine is a product made by man. You plant, you harvest, and you produce. Church can become something like that. All the ingredients can be perfect. It can look and taste good, but wine can intoxicate. It can be dangerous because wine pleases the flesh. The flesh has a powerful appetite. It doesn't crave what is good for it. It craves the instant gratification of pleasure.
You have to remember His love. Success is a great price to pay for so little.

1:4: "…the upright love for thee."

Oh! How sweet it is to please Him, and to desire Him over everything else. He is a jealous God. He won't allow you to love anything more than Him. He desires to be first above all else. His passion for you is undeniable.
Have you, in your quest for success, neglected the one you are serving? Have you truly heard His voice lately? Have you been still long enough to listen?

Can you hear Him?

1:5: "I am black but comely…"

Nothing causes you to examine yourself like being in His presence. *Black* means "empty or void" and *comely* means "righteous".
You know in yourself there is nothing good. You need the loving touch of a Savior just like everyone else. He is the head, and you are the body. So you need the oil of his presence, running down upon you.
Knowing your own weaknesses and inabilities, you must remain under His Kingship at all times. You must allow Him to be Lord overall you do. You must yield it all to Him.

1:5: "…oh ye daughters of Jerusalem…"

Humility is a beautiful character. As you embrace it, others will see His glory. Humility will move you from…

Glory to Glory

…as you change into His image!

Jesus came to minister but He also was a man of quiet refuge. He would often leave the crowd, leave the disciples, and find time to be alone.
He would leave them to draw near to His Father. He found time to be alone.
Do you get away? Even for a little while? Are you able to spend time alone with Him?
You need to purpose in your heart to find time needed…

In His Presence!

1:5: "…as the tents of Kedar, as the curtains of Solomon."

Kedar is such a deep, dark forest. The curtains of Solomon's temple were white and moved easily in the wind.

There is such a difference between your flesh and your spirit. As you surrender to the Holy Spirit, your flesh will diminish and your spirit will thrive. Time spent simply in His presence will cause you to move from Glory to Glory. Time spent in His presence causes us to be…

More like Him.

1:6: "Look not upon me because I am black…"

Time spent in His presence reveals to you your own darkness. As you behold Him in all of His Glory, you will see the real you, the one no one else sees or needs to see.
When you can be honest with yourself and judge yourself according to His Word, you realize that it is Him in you that makes you who you are today! Thank God for the…

Blood of Jesus

That washed your sins away.
The same blood that cleansed the thief, the murderer, and the prostitute, cleansed you. Thank you Jesus!

1:6: "…because the sun (son) has looked upon me…"

Thank God He did! He found you in your sin. He first loved us. He came to you in your place of separation and there He looked at you. He loved you like no one else ever did.
You know it's not you. You know it's Him. He cleansed you. He anointed you. He caused you to be who you are, and to be where you are.
He gets the Glory. Where would you be today if it had not been for Him?

1:6: "…my mother's children were angry with me…"

You were born again as a result of the church. My mother's children would be the people of the church. They were angry (selfish). They may not acknowledge the sacrifices you make…

But Heaven does.

1:6: "…they made me the keeper of the vineyard…"

Have you been seen cooking, cleaning, and laboring in areas of the ministry? Does it seem that your gift has been exchanged for the convenience of others? Could you make a quality decision of faith to believe for someone else to pick up the mantel as keeper of the vineyard, and the church? To find someone who loves you and desires for you to excel in your gifts and callings.
If you will decide to relinquish those time consuming positions, someone else will find an opportunity to serve in their calling. Isn't that how you started? Your opportunity to be free is their opportunity to begin.

1:6: "…my own vineyard, I have not kept."

You need fresh oil, and you need a visitation. You cannot continue to give of yourself without being rejuvenated and refreshed.
In order to be effective we must be continually filled with His precious spirit. Out of your belly shall flow "rivers of living waters".
 Prepare, begin, expect new life, and new ideas. Let all this start with you and accept this challenge of…

The Holy Spirit.

1:7: "Tell me, oh thou whom my soul loveth…"

Be the one who is listening. Listen to His heart. It is His kingdom. He must reign.
New life can only come from Him. He alone can supply your need. Do you need to be energized? Could you be more excited? Do you have expectancy? Or have you decided, like Sarah, that you are past the age to conceive? She was wrong in her opinion of herself. She forgot the voice of the angel that spoke to her. The Lord said she would have a child, and she did.
The Lord says to you,

1:7: "…tell me…where thou feedest…"

Jesus said, "I have meat that you know not of." Jesus knew how to receive from heaven everything His spirit, soul, and body needed. There are certain things you need that no one else can give you. "Deep calleth unto deep,"-Psalm 42:7. There is a place in the spirit where you can go, where your spirit and soul are satisfied.
Jesus was a man in the earth who was in touch with the voice of heaven. Decide to listen, even more, and you might be surprised at what you hear.

1:7: "…where thou makest thy flock to rest at noon…"

He is the great Shepherd and His flock is made up of those who follow Him. They enter into a place of rest because He is lifted up. He is lifted up in their lives like the noon day sun, above everything else. Your spirit needs rest from wondering in this wilderness. As your shepherd, He will lead you beside those beautiful, still waters of provision.

1:7: "…for why should be as one that turneth aside by the flocks of thy companions?"

Some people are content to watch others enter into His presence. Does it seem that you need to portray that you are content? Shouldn't they see you pursuing the one you love and continually being filled with the Spirit? The result of being…

In His Presence.

He Says!

1:8: "If thou know not, oh thou fairest among women…"

He said, "Fairest among women". That's you! *Fair* in Hebrew means "holy". In other words, He is saying, Holiest among many women. Your position in Him is announced.
He says that if you are not aware of who you are in Him, then let Him tell you,

"You are Mine!"

1:8: "…Go thy way forth, by the footsteps of the flock…"

Do not stay where you are. Listen to the voice of your King. You do not need to ask anyone else for permission. Get up on the inside. Get up from your present position, and go forth in your new adventure of life.
Others who have gone on before you who now rest on thrones of Glory have left their footprints in the spirit for you to follow. As you begin this new journey, angels will lead you into your perfect way.

Take the first step toward the new you. Make the decision, to begin again, today.

Begin Again Today!

1:8: "…and feed your kids (the young believers) beside the shepherds tents (the church)."

Be the one that feeds my sheep. As you embrace the unction of The Holy Spirit, you will have what you need. Your vineyard will nourish them. The fruit of your spirit will flourish with new life.

You Will Flourish!

The King Speaks

1:9: "I have compared thee, oh my love…"

Beloved, my thoughts of you are never ending. My plans for you have never changed. I have purposed to fulfill the destiny I have for you.

If you will allow me to order the steps of your future, you will see yourself in the royal position that is yours.

My desire is for you to take your place with me, as the one who wears her crown. Lay down your itinerary, delegate responsibilities, and chase me.

I Can Be Caught.

1:9: "I have compared thee, oh my love to a company of horses in Pharoah's chariots."

The Best of the Best!

I see you, as no one else can. Pharoah's horses were cared for and kept with the highest expectations. No one else had horses that could compare. They were the strongest, the fastest, and the most beautiful.

They were exquisite in value. They never worked in the field. They were considered to be a great treasure. Their potential was without question. Generation after generation proved their worth to the kingdom.

You are exquisite, beautiful, and strong. You have unique potential, like no one else. "Yield to me, my love, and…

"Be!"

1:10: "Thy cheeks are comely, with rows of jewels…"

Jesus says, "You are a reflection of me. As the world looks at you, they will see me. I desire to display my Father's kingdom upon you."
You are to wear the crown my Father has decreed for you to have.

Yield to Me!

1:10: "…Your neck with chains of gold."

Your authority will not be questioned. The rows of jewels upon your cheeks will be a display of my Father's wealth, which is yours. There will be no doubt as to whom you belong to.

"You Belong to Me!"

The chains of gold placed around your neck will announce and display your authority. Those I have entrusted my kingdom to are allowed to possess these gifts!

1:11: "We will make thee, borders (crowns) of gold…"

It is the responsibility of the kingdom to prepare you. As you submit to my will, we will begin. As you trust the prompting of the Holy Spirit, and yield to Him, the anointing will come upon you for Kingship. As Samuel poured the anointing oil upon the head of David, the oil, and the anointing for Kingship will be poured upon you.
You will receive the crown that has been prepared for you.

1:11: "…crowns of gold with studs of silver."

This crown of gold which is to placed upon your head comes with preparation. Silver represents the precious work of The Holy Spirit. We will begin our divine plan.
With refining, preparing and disciplined training, everything will begin to change. As your present life decreases, your new life will increase! I will assign your angels to gather whatever you need.

The Holy Spirit will be present to guide your every step. You will only need to yield. The work is ours to do.

Begin Today! Begin Now!

She Says!

1:12: "While the King sitteth at His table…"

This King possesses the heavens and the earth. It all belongs to Him. It is His, just like a beautiful table set before Him. Anything He desires is His, made available by His Father.
He sits. There is no need for concern. He rests in its abundance. It is His to give to whomever he chooses.
You have been chosen. As you rule under His authority, all of His kingdom will be made available to you. The kingdom assigned to you is under His rule, and He will see to it.
Great is His plan, His vision and His desire, for all to be blessed because of His kingdom!

1:12: "…My spikenard (anointing) sendeth forth the smell (fragrance) there of."

The preciousness of God's gifts, on the King's table, are a display of her royal, magestic heritage.
A holy thing has happened to her. A divine change has manifested. She has received a fresh anointing, a breath of new life and it came from being in His presence. The anointing that brings authority, prosperity, and an abundance of spiritual gifts will manifest. Heavenly gifts, and things money cannot buy, are granted to her by royal decree. She is experiencing…

Change!

1:13: "A bundle of myrrh is my well *Beloved* to me…"

Beloved is a name used to express passion. Out of her worship she is declaring that she is extremely passionate for her King.
She uses the word *myrrh* to describe Him. Myrrh was used as an anointing oil to prepare the body of a loved one for burial.

As you embrace the anointing, you can expect certain things in your life to cease to exist, and to change. Disappointment is an example.

The anointing of your *Beloved* will ignite a new passion in your spirit. It will remove those waste places where life stopped for a season. His anointing will cause them to bloom again!

1:13: "…He shall lie all night between my breast."

You will hold onto the Holy thing he has done for you. As you embrace His love, His anointing, His passion for you, those old places where disappointment remained, will spring forth with new life! He will breathe, and…

You Will Live!

1:14: "My *Beloved* is unto me as a cluster of camphire…"

Camphire means "to cover".

Your *Beloved* is a covering for you. You should announce that He is King over your life. You should

completely surrender to Him. Your past, your present, and your future belong to Him.
Decide to embrace your destiny. Have you? If you have, then you may decree His Word.
Say this:

I receive, and embrace my destiny.

He covers my weaknesses.

He covers my questions.

He covers my enemies.

He covers my needs.

He covers me.

1:14: "…in the vineyards of Engadi."

In your wilderness, in your world, there is a source, and a place where you can receive, and draw living water. You will celebrate the fact that your

will provide.

What was once barren in your life will suddenly burst forth with supernatural provision. As Engadi was a place of safety and serenity for David while he hid from his enemy, Jesus will cover, protect, and provide for you!

He Proclaims!

1:15: "Behold, thou art fair my love, thou art fair…"

Jesus says, "Hear me. Listen to me!"
Close your ears to the opinions of others.
Jesus says:

"I call you Holy.
I call you Mine.
I place your crown upon your head.
I ordain you to reign in your royal position.
I announce to kingdoms of the earth, 'Behold, her royal position of dominion and authority. Her words are my words. Her armies are my armies. They wait for her command. She speaks and legions obey her.'
I anoint you, My Love.
I pour my spirit upon you.

I refresh and recreate your mind, your will and your emotions.

I wash away disappointments.

I restore forgotten dreams.

I breathe into you prophetic promises.

I ordain your footsteps into Kingdom matters.

Today, I say, 'Live again!'"

1:15: "…thou hast dove eyes."

Jesus says:

"I anoint your eyes to receive revelation. You will see what others do not see.

In your position of dominion, you will rule in the spirit.

Kingdoms of this earth will bow to your command.

The Holy Spirit will be your constant companion.

He will be your insight into earthly and kingdom matters.

Focus on your position in me, and my kingdom."

1:16: "Behold, thou art fair, my *Beloved,* yes, pleasant…"

Listen to your King. His love for you is shouted with the voice of many waters, and with the voice that created the heavens and the earth.
He celebrates, He expresses His Holy passion and announces how you please Him. Your willingness, and your life surrendered to Him, allows His kingdom to come, and His will to be done.
You will rule and reign together.

As He is, so are You!

1:16: "…our bed (couch) is green (eternal)."

Jesus says:
 "This is our agreement.
 This is our private vow.
 My Father will be our witness.
 Heaven will be our companion.
 This is your time to grow.
 This is your time to bear fruit.
 This is your time to conceive.

This is your time to deliver.
My gifts and callings are without repentance.
I will fulfill my purpose for your life prepared for you in the beginning, your eternal destiny.
Your gifts are not dead, they are only dormant.
The Holy Spirit will breathe new life into you, and you will birth that Holy Thing in you.
I say, 'Holy Ghost Breathe!
Breathe life into her mind, her body, her spirit, and into her womb!'"

1:17: "The beams of our house are cedar…"

Jesus says:
"You will have structure.
You will have support.
You will have strength.
Kings live in dwellings of cedar, places of provision and protection. As you continue to abide in my

presence, you will have the manifestation of my kingdom. Its presence will surround your life!
Hear my heart!
Decree a thing!
It will be established!"

Believe! Conceive! Deliver!

1:17: "The beams of our house are cedar and the rafters of our house are fir."

Jesus says:
 "Our house, our covenant is supported by the words of my mouth. Our promise is the kingdom of heaven. This is your time. Enjoy the fruit of your labor, it has not been in vain.
 Enter into our house of rest, and labor no more.
 I am the Lord of your harvest.
 Great is your reward.
 Believe for what you desire, and it shall be granted.

As you remain in my presence,
The Holy Ghost will come upon you.
Yield to Him.
Receive His Word and conceive.
It shall come to pass!"

Song of Solomon

Chapter 2

He Speaks!

2:1: "I am the rose of Sharon…"

"I am!"

Have you ever received a promise so big that you knew, in the natural, was impossible?

Think of Sarah. Her heart's desire was to have a child. It had been so long since she was physically able to bear children. She probably already accepted the fact that it was never going to happen for her.

Then one ordinary day, in the midst of cleaning sand from the rugs and preparing meals, angels appeared. They brought with them the word from Jehovah that Sarah would have a child.

The Word of the Lord Came… But How?

Jesus Replied, "Because I Am!"

"I Am!" was a statement made by our God, who parts the Red Sea, who destroys the enemy, who rains manna from the sky and water from a rock. He says He is able. He says…

"I Am!"

Jesus, who walked up to a tomb, and called death out of the grave, says to you that Holy Thing promised to you is not dead! It is only asleep. It is hidden from the world and from destruction. It will live again when…

He Speaks!

When you get a promise like that for a short period of time, you are exhilarated. The future is bright with promise! You can see your gift granted to you from heaven.

Just like the promise was given in Chapter 1, it is given to you by the Holy Spirit. But then your mind begins to overtake your spirit, and the crushing word, "how?" begins to pull you away from the word.

In Chapter 2, your *Beloved* comes to you with the assurance that He is able!

He says…

"I Am!"

2:1:"…the rose of Sharon…"

Sharon is a desert. It is a place of dryness with little sign of life, barren in many ways. Things struggle to live and survive. But there is a rose that actually lives in the desert. It finds life and it flourishes. Psalm 119 repeatedly quotes King David asking the Lord to quicken him with the word.
"Quicken" in the Hebrew language means to bring life, like spring is to the earth. When everything seems dead, suddenly new life appears and signs of new beginnings are everywhere. There is beauty again.

This is what your *Beloved* is saying to you, "I know your dryness. I know your desert."
But if you will embrace His promise, He will cause the word in you to spring forth suddenly with new life.

I Am…the Lily of the Valley

2:1: "I am…the Lily of the Valley."

The Lily was desired for its beauty and fragrance. It could be found in the valleys, surrounded by hills and rocks. There have been times in our lives where you have walked through difficulty. It often seemed like hardship surrounded you more than anything. But in the midst of your valley was the presence of the Holy Spirit, promising you beauty.
Your King is not forgetful of His promises. He even promises you double for your trouble. Houses you didn't build. Wells you didn't dig. (Deut. 6:11)

Prophetic words:

When I speak, dirt comes to life.
When I speak, death comes out of the grave.
Find those promises you have let go of, and Prophesies that you have received.
Believe they are coming to pass.
Believe that I can speak life to them.

2:2: "As the lily among thorns, so is my love among the daughters"

1 John 4:17 says, "…as He is, so are we in the earth."

He sees you prophetically through the blood. All that He is in the earth, is available to you. You are the temple of the Holy Spirit! You possess the Kingdom of God. It abides in you.
In Heaven there is no barrenness. There is no regret or defeat. You possess the very source of life itself. You need to release it into your spirit and live, flourish, and bear much fruit.

She Responds to Him

2:3: "As the Apple Tree among the trees of the wood, so is my *Beloved* among the sons…"

We are surrounded daily with the world. It is full of noise and opinions. She sees Him as the true source of life. She is experiencing her decision to receive from Him and to listen to His voice.
You, like her, need to realize that He alone can touch you with new life, and can bring the oil of gladness you so desperately need. He can restore

the love and passion you experienced in the beginning.

Jeremiah 2:2 says, "…I remember thee, the kindness of thy youth, the love of thine espousals, when thou wentest after me in the wilderness, in a land that was not sown."

2:3:"…I sat down under His shadow with great delight…"

Psalms 37:4 says, "Delight yourself in the Lord and He will give you the desires of your heart."

You are a woman of submission. You have surrendered your life, giving up worldly pleasures to be at His feet.
Many times alone, but in beautiful company, surrounded by the presence of heaven, dreams, visions, and angelic visitations were where you dwelt. Anticipating His presence, where you were alone and in the spirit, He whispered promises to you, and He has not forgotten them, even though you may have.
Responsibilities can take place of intimacy. Yes, you have been on the front line for Him. This is not a retreat, it is a promotion.

2:3: "…and His fruit was sweet to my taste."

Reflecting back on her life, she is expressing gratitude for what He has already done for her. Her submission to His call caused her life to be blessed beyond previous generations.
Like her, you have more knowledge which has produced a sweetness in your life that the world cannot possess.
Deeper submission, greater intimacy can only produce greater blessings and greater fruit.

Life Will Be Sweet!

2:4: "He brought me to the banqueting house…"

The banqueting house is a place of celebration. It is your choice to surrender to His call. He desires to relieve you of front line duty, and to promote you to the house of celebration, where you once again focus on your *Beloved*, and not the battle. He has women assigned to relieve you. Just like the calvary, Heaven is ready to release you from your current obligation.

Officers seldom participate in battle, they delegate. They hear from those in authority and deliver the message.

Can you lay down your sword and sit in His presence and declare?

Thy Will Be Done
Thy Kingdom Come

He Brought Me to His Banqueting House!

2:4: "...and His banner over me was love."

In the midst of battle, a banner over the land will be lifted. It is meant to declare ownership, possession, and victory.

As you surrender to this heavenly promotion, a banner will be lifted over you, and your family, a banner declaring possession and ownership. You belong to the Kingdom of God, and He reigns over you!

Not only is this a declaration of divine love for you, but it is also a banner of victory displayed for your enemies to see.

Jesus Is Lord Over You!

2:5: "Stay me with flagons, comfort me with apples, for I am sick of love."

I Am Love Sick!

All of a sudden passion is ignited again. This is how it used to be. This is how it's supposed to be.

No more struggle, only peace.
No more disappointment, only joy.
No more dryness, only anointing.

The Heavens are open over your life.
The word burst forth in you, bringing new life.
Hope is all around you and anticipation delights you.

Your eyes are once again fixed on Him.

Your ears are listening for His voice.
Your heart anticipates His presence.

"For truly in His presence is fullness of Joy!" - Psalms 16:11

2:6: "His left hand is under my head and His right hand doth embrace me."

Proverbs 3:16: "Length of days is in her right hand; riches and honor are in her left hand."

Promotion in the Kingdom of God brings advantages, blessings, and benefits.

Psalm 91 declares that he who dwells in the secret place shall be blessed and have long life.

Being in His presence and hearing His voice will bring the wisdom to produce the promises in His word.

He said to me:

"If you would have studied law, you would be a lawyer. If you would have studied medicine, you would be a doctor.

But, you chose to study my word, and don't ever compare my wisdom to the world's."

2:7: "I charge you, O ye daughters of Jerusalem, by the roes, and by the hinds of the field, ye stir not up, nor awake my love, till he please."

Now, His contentment is more important to her than her own.
She realizes that what she desires is possible, but only in His time.
The Kingdom of God is available to her, but she must realize He has already ordained His plan for her, and He will see to it in His time.

1 Timothy 6:6: "Godliness with contentment is great gain."

Let Him arrange the circumstance.
Let Him ordain Heaven's protocol.
Let Him get the glory.

2:8: "The voice of my Beloved…"

Numbers 23:21 says "There is the Shout of a King in the camp"

He Speaks
He Rules
He Reigns

His voice is being heard; the voice of many waters, the voice that spoke life in the beginning, the voice that created all there is, and the voice that called Lazarus from the tomb.

2:8 "…behold He cometh leaping upon the mountains and skipping upon the hills."

He leaps with joy. Your mountains, your hills are truly under His feet. "He always causes (you) to triumph!" -2 Corinthians 2:14

Man has always been victorious when under submission to the Kingdom of God; when orders were received and obeyed.

Our Father has put all things under His reign, even your smallest problems!

2:9: "My *Beloved* is like a roe or a young hart…"

She sees Him full of life, and energy, moving without the slightest hint of resistance.

2 Samuel 22:34: "He makes my feet like hinds feet and sets me on my high places."

He gives you the ability to walk in difficult and steep places with the ease of the deer that enjoys the challenge.

2:9: "…behold, He standeth behind our wall…"

… a wall of defense, protection, and security.

2:9: "…He looketh forth at the windows…"

He is observant of His Kingdom. He watches over His *Beloved.* He never moves from His place of Authority.

2:9: "…showing Himself through the lattice."
He is making His presence known!

2:10: "My *Beloved* spake and (He) said unto me:

Rise up my love, my fair one and Come Away!"

She is in His banqueting house. She is where her heart has longed for, and yet, the invitation comes to leave.

Come away from intimacy?
Come away from your presence?

No, come away from where you are and go to your next level of promotion!

2:11: "For lo the winter is past, the rain is over and gone."

2:12: "The flowers appear on the earth; The time of the beginning of the birds has come, and the voice of the turtle (Holy Spirit) is heard in our land."

Wow! His word has quickened her. His word will quicken you!
The winter season is over, and spring is here.
New life is beginning.

Respond to His *Invitation* and *Reign*.

2:13: "The fig tree putteth forth her green figs and the vines with a tender grape give a good smell…"

The fruit of the Spirit is visible in you. The fruit of the Spirit brings new life. You are alive. You are anointed with fresh oil.

Now the very thing He has given you, He wants to use.
Are you willing to do whatever he asks?

2:13: *"…arise my love, and come away."*

Can you leave the comforts of familiarity? Can you simply obey the desires of His Heart? Will you take you place in His Kingdom? Did you mean what you said?

2:14: "Oh my dove (His words of encouragement)..."

Don't lose focus. Don't be distracted. You were prepared for "such a time as this." All of your experiences are valuable resources.
Doves have single vision and they move gently. They don't resist.

2:14: "Thou are in the cleft of the rock, in the secret places of the stairs..."

Don't flinch back. I have you. As my hand covered Moses, my hand covers you. You are anointed to walk in a high place in the position I have ordained for you. In the future I have planned for your place in the Kingdom.

2:14: "...let me see your countenance, let me hear your voice..."

Be alive. Display your royal heritage before me.

Open your mouth. Let the words of my kingdom be heard.

2:14: "…for sweet is thy voice…"

My word is in your mouth.
My word will be heard.

2:14: "…and your countenance is comely."

You Look Like Me!

When they see you, they will see me!

1 John 4:17: "…as He is so are we."

2:15: "Take us the foxes, the little foxes that spoil the vine…"

You are not alone. Listen to the smallest of commands, Don't overlook His instructions.

2:15: "…for our vines have tender grapes."

Be aware, don't quench the Spirit. Walk tenderly before Him. Reverence His presence, and listen. Be slow to speak. Your words will matter!

Her Response

2:16: "My *Beloved* is mine and I am His: He feedeth among the lilies."

She is in neutral.
Perhaps she is anxious about what He will require of her.

She thinks: "I have His Love. I love Him. There are many others possibly more qualified than me."

And She Says To Him

2:17: "Until the day break and the shadows flee away, turn my *Beloved* and be thou like a roe or a young hart upon the mountains of Bethar."

"Bethar" means "separation."

Is she too comfortable where she is?
Can she not trust Him, and His plan for her?
What causes you to hesitate?

Chapter 3

Have you ever stood in the presence of your *Beloved,* knowing in your spirit what He asked you to do, and said, "No"?

I have. Years ago, we lived in the hill country, happily secluded from the world. Our children were in home-school. We were in the middle of 35,000 acres of wildlife, overlooking a beautiful lake. We began to feel a tug on our hearts that things were going to change. Then one Sunday morning in church, I heard the Holy Spirit say, "You're going to go to Splendora (home), and offer your help."

How could I leave the security of this home and take my children back to where Gene and I grew up? Too many worldly influences! So, I went to prayer. I wrestled with my flesh, and my flesh won. I remember during prayer announcing to the Lord, "No. I'm not going." I said to him, "I know I will have to face your judgment, but I will not take my children there", and I waited for His response.

He did speak, but he did not judge me. He did not rebuke
me. Instead, He gave me a promise.

He gave me Isaiah 54:13, which says, "Your children shall be taught of the Lord, and great will be their peace!"

So, I surrendered to His will. Circumstances gently moved us, and it was fun!

My children are mature adults now with families of their own. Has life been perfect? No. But I can truly say, this many years later, my children are taught of the Lord, and great is their peace!

Praise The Lord!

I chose to surrender!

3:1: "By night, on my bed, I sought Him whom my soul loveth…"

There are seasons in your life when it seems that He is not as close to you as He used to be.

Could it be you became too comfortable in the midst of all of your blessings, and too comfortable to stay close to Him?

Have you missed divine opportunities to walk with Him in high places? Is it easier to just enjoy the bountiful pleasures He brings to your life?

He has a mission and not even His love for you will allow Him to cease to Reign over His kingdom.

She realizes that she spoke out of her soulish realm, refusing His call, and remaining still. It brought her emptiness and a void only His presence could fill.

3:1: "… I sought Him, but I found Him not."

He is not in your traditions and religions. He is not going to stay within your comfort zone. He must be about His Father's business.

What does it take to find Him?
Jeremiah 29:13 says, "You will find me when you seek me with your whole heart."

He must be first in your life. Your love for Him has to be before everything. He has to have those whose heart is one with Him; one in Spirit, and one in purpose, those with whom He can share His desire.

3:2: "I will rise NOW and Go about the city in the streets and in the broad ways. I will seek Him whom my soul loveth. I sought Him but I found Him not."

The decision to answer the call on your life is a personal decision. No one else can do it for you. It requires a sincere motive to please Him and Him alone.
It also requires complete obedience to His instruction. You are not given the opportunity to come to Him on your terms, you must come to him completely; in total surrender. Until you do, He will wait!

3:3: "The watchmen that go about the city found me…"

He will never just leave you behind. You have angels assigned to you.

He heard her, but He knew she was speaking from her soul, her emotions, and not her spirit.

The Word says in Matthew 26:41, "Our spirits indeed are willing, but our flesh is weak."

So, you have back up! Heaven's army will minister to you. The Holy Spirit will encourage you and "you can do all things through Him, who strengthens you!" –Philippians 4:13.

3:3 "…they found me: to whom I said, saw ye Him, whom my soul loveth?"

Sometimes the human side of you can get the better of you. But He knows your potential. His passion will cause Him to allow a hunger and a thirst. When you are truly hungry, and thirsty, a fresh out pouring of the Holy Spirit will come upon you, still drawing you deeper and deeper into His presence.

3:4: "It was but a little while that I passed from them, but I found Him whom my soul loveth…"

Seasons come and go. This season of hunger and thirst for her was brief. She left the past and turned her heart towards the future: her future with Him. She decided that whatever He asks of me, that will I do.

Be it unto me, according to your word.

Total surrender to the decision made. I will wear His crown.

I Will Wear His Crown!

3:4: "…I found Him whom my soul loveth, I held Him, and would not let Him go…"

Seasons of hunger and thirst allow you to dig deeper. They also create vessels able to contain more; more of Him.

The more of us that He possesses, the more priceless He becomes. You will not let go of Him, not for anything or anyone.

You hold onto all the wisdom, all the knowledge, and all the experiences that brought you to where you are today.

To reign in His Kingdom is to be as He is in this world.

Kingdom Minded!

3:4: "…I held Him and I would not let Him go until I had brought Him into my mother's house, and into the chamber of her that conceived me."

You are a product of His church, His Bride. This Bride is a gift to your *Beloved.* A gift being prepared for that glorious day when His Father says: "Son, go and get your bride!"

Living in the Spirit causes you to be Kingdom minded. You become aware of the Body of Christ and their needs.

The Spirit of God, the Holy Spirit wants and desires to touch and prepare you for this royal celebration.

You will be without spot or wrinkle. You will be dressed in fine linen, prepared to be one with Him in His kingdom.

You Will Never Let Go Of Him!

3:5: "I charge you, oh ye daughters of Jerusalem, by the roes and by the hinds of the fields that you stir not upon awake my love, until He please."

She is shouting to ministers, to workers, in the Father's house, in His Kingdom to listen, listen to the voice of the Holy Spirit.

Listen to what He wants. Be aware of His Instructions.

He is jealous over His Bride. He is jealous over His church. He will have His way. It is all His in divine time, she is ready. Are you?

The Great Crowd of Witnesses Speak

3:6-11: "Who is this that cometh out of the wilderness like pillars of smoke, perfumed with myrrh and frankincense, with all powders of the merchant?
7 Behold his bed, which is Solomon's; threescore valiant men are about it, of the valiant of Israel.
8 They all hold swords, being expert in war: every man hath his sword upon his thigh because of fear in the night.
9 King Solomon made himself a chariot of the wood of Lebanon.
10 He made the pillars thereof of silver, the bottom thereof of gold, the covering of it of purple, the midst thereof being paved with love, for the daughters of Jerusalem.
11 Go forth, O ye daughters of Zion, and behold king Solomon with the crown wherewith his mother crowned him in the day of his espousals, and in the day of the gladness of his heart."

The Promise

Here in this beautiful scene, the King of Glory and the hand maiden of Song of Solomon celebrate their betrothal. They are displaying their mutual promises to each other.

This is His day; the day of great reward. She is His reward. No price too great to pay. Today He celebrates her surrender.

All of Heaven looks upon her as she enters. Her beauty is a reflection of His glory. She has left behind her questions. She has abandoned her fears. She has surrendered to Him and to his will.

He Crowns Her!

A Vision to Behold
Chapter 4

The King Speaks

4:1: "Behold, Thou art fair, My Love, Behold, Thou art fair…"

The decision has been made to surrender to His will. You have allowed The Holy Spirit to prepare you for your destiny and because you did, He will ordain your steps towards your future.
Look who you have become; a vision to behold. You are one with Him; one in purpose and in spirit. You must see yourself in the spirit and not through the eyes of man.

John 1:11: "He came unto His own, and His own received Him not."

The creator of the universe was not recognized by common man. The Son of God, our Messiah, the lover of your soul, wasn't even known. But, all of Heaven celebrates Him every minute of every day.

You, His *Beloved,* may not be recognized by people, but Heaven celebrates you. Begin to look at yourself in the spirit. Begin to put on royalty. See the angels bringing to you everything he has promised.

I called you

I'll make a way

I'll go before you

I'll give you the treasures of heaven

4:1:"…thou hast dove eyes within thy locks…"

The first image described of your new character is your eyes.
No longer are you only a wife, daughter, sister, and grandmother. You are now His! You must begin to look at yourself to see what He sees. He sees royalty, and you must see it.
It's not pride. It is respect for Him. It's respect for what you've become because of Him.

Doves are said to have single vision. They focus on one thing. You have the eyes of a dove. You have the ability to focus on Him, and His word.
His word says:

> *You are the Bride of Christ*
> *He has given you His Name*
> *He has given you His Authority*
> *Angels will Hearken to your Words*
> *Take your Place; Rule and Reign*

4:1: "…thy hair is as a flock of goats that appear from Mount Gilead."

Your hair, in the Word represents a person's strength.
Women are strong. Their ability to bring forth life and to nurture is a gift from God.

Your strength is a beautiful part of your character. In the natural, you may be weak, but in the spirit you are very strong. Your decision to submit to His calling is a result of your strength. When others waver in their faith in Him, you remain faithful. You are the one who believes and trusts in His presence and ability.

Your strength comes from knowing His word. It comes from hearing His voice, and standing upon every promise.

Mount Gilead was a special place where the animals were kept in preparation for the temple sacrifices.

Your life has become a sacrifice for Him. Your heart's desire is to do whatever it takes to please Him. Your purpose and your passion, is for Him only.
4:2: "Thy teeth are like a flock a flock of sheep that are even shorn…"

Your teeth represent your ability to eat, to chew, and digest the Word.

Hebrews 5:14: "Strong meat belongeth to them that are of full age, even those who by reason of use have their senses exercised to discern both good and evil.

As you read his word, it is life to you. You read it and it becomes Rhema. It isn't ink on paper, His words are life. You read and allow it to transform you.

Your teeth are even! You have a balanced revelation of the word, and it brings royalty and humility to you. You know that you are who you are because of who He is.

4:2: "…every one beareth twins…"

Animals that give birth to twins are a greater value to the owner because they produce more in their lifetime than the average.
Look at yourself. See the potential He sees. Dream big. Take the chance. Prepare for success. It's not too late, and it's not too early. His timing for you is now.
Listen to the spirit. Believe you can. Believe you will.

Just Believe!

4:2: "…and none is bare, among them."

You will not fail

You will succeed
Today is your day
Begin now!

Your footsteps into the plan have already been ordained. Every door already opened. Every need already met.

Dream Big & Go!
Expect Something Wonderful!

4:3: "Thy lips are like a thread of scarlet and thy speech is comely…"

Not only is the Word going to be Rhema to you, but you will speak in dominion and authority. Your words will bring deliverance to those in captivity. You are the one anointed. You are the one representing His Kingdom. As you speak to situations, spirits that have held people in bondage will have to obey your command. As you speak, angels assigned to your mission will carry out your commands. Your words of royal decree will manifest.

Psalms 103:20: "Bless the Lord, ye his angels that excel in strength, that do his commandments, hearkening unto the voice of His word."

4:3: "…thy temples are like a piece of pomegranate within thy locks."

Your temples represent your thoughts. You will be kingdom minded. You won't think like other people think.
In your situation and other situations, you will have the answer. The answer is His word. You know that the Word says, "With God, nothing shall be impossible…"-Luke 1:37.

You won't be swayed by tears and fears. You will be the one focused on His promises, His faithfulness, and His ability to do what He said He would do.

Pomegranate seeds are clear with a red tint. Your thoughts and your wisdom will be clear to you because they have been washed in the Blood of Jesus.

4:4: "Thy neck is like a tower of David…"

David, who was a king, was also known as a great warrior. You are seen beautifully dressed in royal apparel, but you have fought some battles and as you did, you towered over your enemy. Every battle and every victory brought increase to your reputation as a great warrior.
Now, as you have been granted promotion, as you reign in your place of authority, you will help others win their battles. Your experiences have brought you great wisdom. Wisdom He can use as he manifests his kingdom here in the earth.

4:4: "…built for an armory where there hangs a thousand bucklers, all shields of mighty men."

Psalm 91:4: "…His truth shall be thy shield and buckler."

You have been built. You have been prepared for now. Everything you need to know has already been deposited in you. You will have the answer. You are mighty in valor and in strength. Victory will come easily to you. Wisdom is the primary thing, and you have it!

Proverbs 4:7: "Wisdom is the principal thing; therefore get wisdom: and with all thy getting, get understanding."

4:5: "Thy two breasts are like two young roes that are twins, which feed among the lilies."

Lilies are pure white flowers that represent the mature believer.
Song of Solomon 2:16 says, "My beloved is mine, and I am His: he feedeth among the lilies." Who do you receive from? This description of the bride declares that you are able to receive from others who are mature, and who represent the kingdom. Because of discipline and commitment, ministry is easy for you. Just like a mother is able to give the necessary life-giving milk to her young, you are able to give life-giving wisdom to those who are young, and hunger for the things of God.

4:6: "Until the day break, and the shadows flee away, *I will* get to the mountain of myrrh, and to the hill of frankincense."

Previously in the earlier stage of her walk with the King, she was in love. She embraced Him, but she was hesitant to follow Him completely.

In verse 2:17 she said the same thing but asked Him to go without her. For whatever reason, she could not abandon all that had become familiar to her. But now, her commitment and love for Him has caused her to just surrender and go.

Myrrh is used as an anointing oil in preparation for burial. The former plans for life are offered as a sacrifice, and as a gift for her *Beloved.*

Frankincense is an incense burnt for worship. When you give yourself as a gift, it is the highest form of worship.

It is Truly All About You!
And
It is Truly All About Him!
He Speaks!

4:7: "Thou art fair, my love, There is no spot in thee."

Again, His words are words that no one else speaks to you. No one else calls you Holy, but He does. He sees you in the spirit draped in righteousness, and crowned in glory.

He says to you:

There is no Spot in You.

He is saying that you have grown and you are complete in Him. Your focus, your words, your thoughts and your ministry are all complete. It is your time.

Now He Asks Again

4:8: "Come with me from Lebanon, *My Spouse* with me from Lebanon…"

Deep calleth unto deep, My Bride.

4:8: "…look from the top of Amana (integrity), from the top of Sheneir (strength), from the top of Herman (power)"

4:8: "…look upon the lions' dens and the mountains of the leopards."

My *Beloved,* you have taken your place. Now that you have chosen to wear my crown, the enemy will no longer be able to hide from you.
Because of your strength, because of the anointing your life now carries, you will reign and bring deliverance to those in my Kingdom.

Lions represent the enemy that is bold and easily seen. They make noise as they go about, seeking who they can devour.
Leopards hide and are rarely seen. They are the enemy that hides in generational curses.
But you have been given my name, and in my authority, they will be exposed and defeated.

4:9: "Thou hast ravished my heart, my sister, my spouse, thou hast ravished my heart…"

You have caused my heart to beat with excitement, with expectation. I have waited for this day. I have loved you. I have wanted you to know me. Not through the eyes of man, but through your own eyes.
To be the strong leader, to be one with me, in my Kingdom!

4:9: "…with one of your eyes, with one chain of thy neck."

There is more to see; I will show you more.
There is more to gain; I will give it to you.

4:10: "How fair is your love for me, my sister, my spouse. How much better is your love than wine and the smell of thine ointments than all spices!"

How holy is your love for me? It alone has caused you to become a strong leader among many. We are one. Your love for me, and your love for my word has caused you to become who you are. It is a gift. The ascension of your worship is sweeter than any other gift.

4:11: "Thy lips, oh my spouse drop as the honeycomb drop, honey and milk are under thy tongue…"

Your words fall on me like the sweetest of honey. When you come to me in worship, it draws me to you.

4:11: "…your garments like the smell of Lebanon."

Remaining in my presence will move you from Glory to Glory.

"…we all, with open face, beholding as in a glass, the glory of the Lord, are changed into the same image from *Glory to Glory,* even as by the spirit of the Lord." 2 Corinthians 3:18

4:12: "A garden enclosed is my sister, my spouse, a spring shut up, a fountain sealed."

4:13: "Your plants are an orchard of pomegranates with pleasant fruits, camphire and spikenard."

Your love is a gift, and I can receive what my heart desires.

Keep your heart for me and protect it from the world.

4:14: "Spikenard and saffron, calamus and cinnamon with all these of frankincense, myrrh, and aloes, with all the chief spices."

4:15: "A fountain of gardens, a well of living waters, and streams from Lebanon."

You will flourish, as our garden of fellowship grows. The gifts of the spirit will multiply, and the increase will flow from Heaven.

She Says

4:16: "Awake, O north wind; and come, thou south; blow upon my garden, that the spices thereof may flow out. Let my *Beloved* come into his garden, and eat his pleasant fruits."

She calls Him her *Beloved.* She referred to Him before as the one her soul loved.

This is an expression of her maturity and passion.

She has found purpose, passion, and…

His Presence!

Chapter 5

He Says, "I am!"

5:1: "I am…"

In the presence of His beautiful bride, the King of Kings decrees, "I am."
It was He who caused you to be who you are. He gets the glory. He knows your potential and knows what you need to achieve it.
The intimate attention given to you by the Holy Spirit has prepared you for now, for this time in your life. It is not you, it is the glory of God.

5:1: "I am come into my garden, my sister, my spouse…"

He calls you "His garden." He can enjoy His reward. His thoughts, His plans, His desires are manifested in you; a place of pleasure.
His calling you "sister" proclaims the strength of your relationship. His calling you "my spouse" proclaims the devotion of your heart. He knows that you will share His kingdom.

5:1: "…I have gathered my myrrh with my spice; I have eaten my honeycomb with my honey; I have drunk my wine with my milk; Eat, oh friends; drink yea, drink abundantly, O beloved."

This is a picture of a celebration. Your Beloved King is gazing at you; expressing all that He sees in you. He is saying for all to hear. I know her. Receive from her. Drink, Drink abundantly. My word is in her, My spirit is in her.

She Speaks

5:2: "I sleep, but my heart waketh…"

It is no longer I, but He that liveth in me. I am not who I used to be. My spirit is awake and I am alive, more than ever. The past is past. I am alive in Him.

5:2: "…it is the voice of "my" *Beloved* that knocketh, saying, Open to me, my sister, my love, my dove, my undefiled…"

The world isn't speaking to your spirit. It is the King of Kings, The Lord of Lords. It is He who is calling you to walk in your high place. It is He who sees you in all your glory as His righteousness drapes over you and His glory crowns you.

My Sister- strong one
My Love- one in spirit
My Dove- faithful
My Undefiled- without spot

He Speaks

5:2: "…for my head is filled with dew and my locks with the drops of the night."

He is the one who intercedes for you. Who enquires of the Holy Spirit. Who goes to the Father. Who sends forth His angels.
His head, wet from the dew of the night. Time spent interceding for you, His *Beloved.*

Her Response:

5:3: "I have put off my coat; how shall I put it on? I have washed my feet; how shall I delfile them?

It seems, when He calls us, it happens when circumstances are not of our choice. We hesitate, desiring a more favorable time, but again, we need to trust Him.

5:4: "My Beloved put in His hand by the hole of the door and my bowels (spirit) were moved for Him."

If you look at the hand of your *Beloved,* you see the scar from the nail. The price we may pay to obey Him will never compare to the price He paid for us.

Our flesh is often weak and hesitant but our spirit is awake to His voice, and we should desire, more than anything, to please Him.

5:5: "I rose up to open to my *Beloved,* and my hands dropped with myrrh and my fingers with sweet smelling myrrh, upon the handles of the lock.

When you are led by the spirit, denying your own flesh, pushing past your own doubts and hesitancies, you will then experience the anointing He has placed on you.
Your hands represent the work, and the ministry He has called you to and it will literally be

saturated in the anointing. Those things locked away, kept away, will be granted. The door will open for you.

5:6: "I opened to my *Beloved;* but my *Beloved* had withdrawn Himself and was gone: my soul failed when He spake…"

We sometimes take our time, or hesitate, when we hear Him speak. I have discovered that it isn't because I question Him, but because I question myself.

5:6: "…I sought Him but I could not find Him; I called Him, but He gave me no answer."

Jeremiah 2:2 says "I remember the, the kindness of thy youth, the love of thine espousals, when thou wentest after me in the wilderness in a land that was not sown."

Believe it! He enjoys your attention. If He is not immediately at your beck and call, chase Him! He will let you find Him!

5:7: "The watchmen that went about the city found me, they smote (touched) me…"

The word smote means to gently apply pressure to conform to an image; like the potter who gently forms the clay.
We know we have not reached perfection, yet.

Hebrews 13:17 says, "Obey leaders and submit to authority… they keep watch over you and must give an account…"

Expect and be confident that He will send to you those who are capable to accomplish for you, whatever you need.

5:7: "…the keeper of the walls (those the Lord has placed in position for you) took my veil away from me."

Sometimes we can't see what others can see. They will be anointed to speak into your life; to direct your footsteps and to speak, revelation into you. You are never alone. All of heaven is prepared to meet your every need. You will have the wisdom and knowledge you need in every decision made. Their wisdom will bring you revelation.

5:8: "I charge you, Oh daughters of Jerusalem, if you find my *Beloved,* that you tell Him, that I am sick of Love (I am love sick)."

All of this is so wonderful. To be love sick means that you are unable to act normal. It soon becomes impossible to keep all of this revelation, to yourself. You will hear yourself speaking about Him, sharing this new passion that has been ignited in you!

Observers Speak

5:9: "What is thy *Beloved* more than another *Beloved?* O thou fairest among women? What is thy *Beloved* more than another *Beloved* that thou dost so charge us?"

Your passion for Him will cause others to desire to know Him.
Out of your spirit will flow words that will touch them. You will hear yourself saying this:

She Answers Them

5:10: "My *Beloved* is white and ruddy, the chiefest among ten thousand."

His Love is so pure and sincere. He knows you. He embraces every flaw. He restores and adorns.
He is passionate about you and your life.
There is no one else who loves you as He does. No one else is as passionate about you as He is. He is the only one.

5:11: "His head is as the most fine gold…"
Gold represents divinity. He is the King of Kings and the Lord of Lords.

5:11: "…His locks (hair) are bushy and black as ravens."

He is not weary and aged. His hair is not thinning.
It is healthy, shiny, and bushy.
It is not turning gray, it is black as the ravens.
He is forever young and strong!

5:12: "His eyes are as the eyes of doves, by the rivers of water, washed with milk and fitly set."

His eyes do not express disappointment in you. They are full of life and sparkle. They express the word spoken over you. His eyes are fitly set on you and He will not be distracted. You have captured His attention.

5:13: "His cheeks are as a bed of spices, as sweet flowers, His lips like lilies, dropping sweet smelling myrrh."

Can you see His face? His eyes are compassionate, and focused on you, knowing everything there is to know about you. There is nothing hidden from Him. He sees you with excitement and energy, ready to do a beautiful work in you.
As you look at Him, His expression is one that caused you to desire Him even more. His words spoken to you touch your spirit, causing you to leap in faith.

5:14: "His hands are as gold rings set with beryl…"

His wealth is apparent. His ability to do what He says is without question. Like a gold ring set with rare precious stones, He is like no one else.

5:14: "…His belly is a bright ivory overlaid with sapphires."

His belly represents His spirit. King Solomon made himself a throne of ivory and covered it with gold and precious stones.
He is the King of Kings and will be the King over your life.
As you commit yourself to reign in your glorious position as the Bride of Christ, He will reign over you and your life as the King of the Universe.

5:15: "His legs are as pillars of marble; set upon sockets of fine gold…"

He will never grow weak in the knees. His strength and endurance is without question.
He will be strong for you in any type of situation you may encounter.

5:15: "…His countenance is as Lebanon, excellent as the cedars."

Lebanon, as we stated in Isaiah 35:1-2, represents the Glory and majesty of the Kingdom of Heaven.

Isaiah 35:1-2:"The wilderness and the solitary place shall be glad for them; and the desert shall rejoice and blossom as the rose.(2) It shall blossom abundantly, and rejoice even with joy and singing: the glory of Lebanon shall be given unto it…"

His face and His expression is a beautiful reflection of the glory and majesty of heaven.

Cedars are tall and strong. They were used in construction because of their durability. Jesus is above all else and there is none to compare.

He rejoices over you with singing. Your love and devotion brings Him much joy and reason to rejoice.

Isaiah 62:5: "…as the bridegroom rejoiceth over the bride, so shall thy God rejoice over thee."

5:16: "His mouth is most sweet: yea He is all together lovely…"

No one else will ever speak to you the way Jesus will. His love and compassion for you will always be expressed by him. He is truly, the Lover of your soul.

5:16: "…this is my Beloved, and this is my friend, oh ye daughters of Jerusalem."

The world will ask, as in verse 5:9, why is your *Beloved* more than another *Beloved.* They will want to know, why Jesus is different from anyone else.

As you speak His name, as you tell of His wonderful love, as you reveal that He is the King of the universe, creator of everything that exists, His majestic presence will be felt, and they will experience this glorious king for themselves.

Observers Speak

Chapter 6

6:1: "Whither is thy *Beloved* gone, oh thou fairest among women? Whither is thy *Beloved* turned aside? that we may seek Him with thee."

When others see and hear your love expressed for your *Beloved,* they will begin to desire what you have.
He will use your love for Him to touch them.
We all have a spirit that is empty without Him.

She Speaks

6:2: "My *Beloved* is gone down into His garden to the beds of spices to feed in the gardens and to gather lilies."

You will have the answer to their questions and wisdom will speak through you, and when they experience His presence, they will never forget it.

6:3: "I am my *Beloved's,* and my *Beloved* is mine: He feedeth among the lilies."

You can lift your hands in praise. You can rejoice and declare you know Him! He abides with those that truly love Him.

He decrees!

6:4: "Thou art beautiful, oh my love, as Tirzah, comely as Jerusalem, terrible (awesome) as an army with banners."

The Hebrew definition for Tirzah means: "She is my delight", and "favorable."
You are a delight to Him. You are as beautiful as the city of Jerusalem and your victorious life is cause for a celebration in His kingdom.

6:5: "Turn away thine eyes from me, for they have over come me…"

Have you ever considered that you could influence the King of the universe and that your presence and devoted attention would touch Him? The fact that you are one in spirit with Him is kingdom protocol. You have the mind of Christ; you think the thoughts of heaven. You are reigning in your position, in your high place.

He hears you! He listens! Talk to Him!

6:5: "…thy hair is as a flock of goats that appear from Gilead."

Gilead was where the priest kept the sacred animals. They were set apart to be sacrificed in the temple as an obedient act to the Word.
He says to you, "your strength is a result of your daily sacrifice"; your willingness to surrender to His will.

6:6: "Thy teeth are as a flock of sheep which go up from washing, whereof everyone beareth twins, and there is not one barren among them."

6:7: "As a piece of a pomegranate are thy temples within thy locks."

6:8: "There are three score queens and four score concubines and virgins without number."

Your place in the kingdom of God surrounds you with a family of believers. You are not alone. You are part of a glorious kingdom; a kingdom with innumerable angels and with the presence of the Holy Spirit.

6:9: "My love, my undefiled is but one, she is the only one of her mother, she is the choice of one of her that bare her…"

The Bible says that many are called but few are chosen. (Matthew 20:16)
Not everyone chooses to answer His call, but He is declaring that you are the one that heard His voice. You are the one who chose to surrender to His call.

You chose to wear His crown!
The Great Crowd of Witnesses Speak

6:9: "…the daughters saw her, and blessed her, the queens and the concubines, and they praised her."

The body of Christ, the church will recognize the anointing on your life. When the presence of God surrounds your life, you become someone that others desire to draw from.

6:10: "Who is she that looketh forth as the morning? Fair as the moon and clear as the sun…"

Fair As The Moon and Clear As The Sun!

Just like the moon's light is a reflection of the sun, you have become a reflection of Him. Sunlight removes darkness. You are as radiant as the sun. When the world sees you, they will see Jesus.

You Are a Beautiful Reflection of Him!

6:10: "Who is (she)…?"

A new you, with a fresh anointing placed upon your spirit; a new endowment of energy and strength; a new purpose and a new determination to work in your divine destiny. Old things are forgotten and left upon the alter. It is a gift given to Him.

6:10: "Who is (she) that looketh forth as the morning…?"

It's a new day for you! Darkness is past and the sun is rising upon a new day, and a new season for you. Choose to hear the birds singing. Choose to notice new opportunities springing up for you, divine appointments leading you on a bright and clear path.

6:10: "…clear as the sun…"

You are a reflection of Him. As He is in the earth so are you (1 John 4:17). As the moon reflects the light of the sun, you are a reflection of Him. He is high and lifted up with a name above all names. You are the head and not the tail; above and not beneath.

6:10: "…terrible as an army (of believers) with banners."

Terrible means awesome. Your life, your destiny! You are awesome! You are surrounded by the family of faith. You are surrounded by the angels of heaven. Wherever your feet shall tread, you will possess the land. You are invincible!

You are awesome; as powerful as an army, parading, and celebrating victories while banners wave over you, declaring, wherever you go…

"Jesus is Lord!"

She Declares

6:11-12: "I went down into the garden of nuts to see the fruits of the valley, and to see whether the the vine flourished and the pomegranates budded. (12) Or ever I was aware, my soul made me like the chariots of Amminadib."

As you begin your new adventure you will discover your own strength and ability. Like chariots swift and beautiful, you will move with ease and much success will be yours to enjoy.

6:13: "Return, return, O Shulamite; return, return, that we may look upon thee. What will ye see in the Shulamite? as it were the company of two armies."

People will desire to receive from you. Favor will surround you. As you move, you will move in the spirit, and we will be one.

John 17:11: "…Holy Father, keep through thine own name those whom thou hast given me, that they may be one, as we are."

We are one!

Chapter 7

Begin!

God is able to make all grace abound towards you, so that in everything you are sufficient.

He Speaks!

7:1: "How beautiful are your feet with shoes…"

Now you are ready! Ready to go! So know this, your shoes are uniquely prepared just for you. Just like a pair of new shoes that excite you, my calling for you will be just as exciting.
Not worn-out, not the wrong size, style or color. Customized to your expectations, and beautifully fit.
Shoes prepared for this season in your life; prepared for your new adventure.

7:1: "…the joints of thy thighs are like jewels…"

Jewels represent beauty and wealth? Your thighs are actually a major source of your strength.

So it is obvious that your strength is a beautiful character and it is also a great value to the kingdom of God.

7:1: "…the work of the hands of a cunning workman."

Cunning means: wisdom, understanding and knowledge.

Everything you put your hand to will prosper. Your wisdom, understanding, and knowledge will bring you success.

7:2: "Thy navel is like a round goblet which wanteth not liquor…"

You have the Holy Spirit and you have the fruit of the spirit. You are prepared and you are able to do what He has called you to do.

7:2: "…thy belly is like a heap of wheat set about with lilies."

You have the Bread of Life, His word, and He will surround you with those who are full of wisdom to assist you in whatever you need.

7:3: "Thy two breasts are like two young roes that are twins."

You are going to bear more fruit than you ever imagined.

Think Big!
Dream Big! Expect More!

7:4: "Thy neck is a tower of ivory…"

Your submission to the will of God is a beautiful example for others to watch and see.

7:4: "…thine eyes like fish pools in Heshbon, by the gate Bath-rabbin…"

Your devotion and focus on the kingdom of God is beautiful. You will leap over walls…with ease. (Psalms 18:29)

7:4: "…thy nose is as the tower of Lebanon which looketh toward Damascus."

Breathe In.

You have the Spirit and you have discernment. It resides in you. The Glory of God surrounds you and will lead you into my perfect will.

7:5: "Thine head upon thee is like carmel…"

Your mind is made up. You have made your decision, the victory is yours to have.

7:5: "…and the hair of your head is like purple…"

See yourself, as my royal companion. Walk in your divine position.

7:5: "…the king is held in galleries."

See me with you. Expand your borders, stretch yourself, believe, and go.

Begin!

7:6: "How fair, how pleasant art thou, oh love for delights."

Your beautiful spirit pleases me. It causes me to rejoice. You bring me much pleasure.

7:7: "This, thy stature is like a palm tree, and thy breast to clusters of grapes."

Like palm trees in a desert, you are a source of life He can share. You are rare and you are a gift to others.

7:8-9 "I said, I will go to the palm tree, I will take hold of the boughs there of now also thy breasts shall be as clusters of the vine, and the smell of thy nose like apples. (9) And the roof of your mouth, like the best wine for my *Beloved*, (the church), that goeth down sweetly…"

He will use you. You are in His hands. You are one.

Now, begin. You will see increase, and you will produce much for the kingdom.

The words of your mouth will be anointed. My *Beloved*, my church, will receive fresh revelation from you.

7:9: "…causing the lips of those who are asleep to speak."

The anointing He has placed on your life is going to wake up His Bride who has surrendered to her comfort. She will receive. She will awaken to His voice, and she will speak.

She Speaks

7:10: "I am my *Beloved's* and His desire is toward me."

Decree over yourself who you are!

Say this:

I belong to the King of Kings.
I am royalty in His kingdom.
He need not search for companionship.
His desire is toward me.

7:11-12: "Come, my *Beloved,* let us go forth into the field: let us lodge in the villages. (12) Let us get up early to the vineyards, let us see if the vine flourishes, whether the tender grape appear, and the pomegranate bud forth

There will I give thee, my love."

It is your love for Him that will cause you to go. It will cause you to step into responsibilities. It will cause you to invest your self into others.

This is your gift of love, to Him.

7:13: "The mandrakes give a smell, and at our gates are all manner of pleasant fruits, new and old, which I have laid up for thee,

"Oh my love!"

Say:
I give you everything. I will obey and begin. I give you all of my past, and all of my future. It is a gift to you. I lay it on the alter. May the fragrance of my sacrifice bring pleasure to you, my king.

She Speaks

Chapter 8

8:1-2: "Oh that thou were, as my brother that sucked the breast of my mother. When I should find thee without, I would kiss thee, yea I should not be despised. (2) I would lead thee and bring thee into my mother's house, who would instruct me? I would cause thee to drink of spiced wine of the juice of my pomegranate."

The law requires her not to show public affection. But if he were actually her brother she could kiss him. She would boldly display her love for him, and she would not be ashamed. She is experiencing the desire to share with others what she now has.

8:3: "His left hand should be under my head and His right hand should embrace me."

She will place her life in His hands. In His left hand are riches and in His right hand is life.

In Him, I will live, move, and abide.

8:4: "I charge you oh daughters of Jerusalem, that you stir not up, nor awake my love until He please."

She will not allow others to disrupt what she has found in Him. She is content in what He has done in her. She is content in who she is in Him.

He Says

8:5: "Who is this that cometh *up* from the wilderness, leaning upon her *Beloved…?*

You have stepped out of the past, out of preparation. You have learned that He alone is the source of life. You no longer look to others for approval; you look to Him. Lean on His promise, lean on His strength, *Beloved,* lean on Him.

He says:

8:5-6: "…I raised thee up, under the apple tree, there thy mother brought thee forth; there she brought thee forth, that bare thee. (6) Set me as a seal upon thine heart, as a seal upon thine arm…

...for my love is strong as death; my jealousy as cruel as the grave, the coal there of are coals of fire which have a most vehement flame." His love for you will not grow cold. The flames of His passion will consume every obstacle before you as you go.

He says:

"Commit yourself to me. Commit yourself to our future. Commit yourself to the kingdom of God."

8:7: "Many waters cannot quench love, neither can the floods drown it, if a man would give all the substance of His house for love, it would utterly be contemned."

"I will be faithful to our vows of commitment. Nothing will distract or discourage me."

She Says

8:8: "We have a little sister, she has no breast. What shall we do for our sister in the day when she shall be spoken for?"

Now you have been made aware of the need of others. Your sensitivity has matured to look beyond your own needs. You have become kingdom minded.

8:9: "If she be a wall, *we will* build upon her a palace of silver: and if she be a door, *we will* enclose her with boards of cedar."

She Says:

"I know now that I can do all things through You because You love me. It is not me, nor my ability. It is You!"

8:10: "I am a wall, and my breasts are like towers: then was I in His eyes as the one that found favor."

You are able. You can do all things through Christ who strengthens you. You have found favor in the eyes of God.

8:11: "Solomon had a vineyard at Baal-hamon; he let out the vineyard to keepers: everyone for the fruit there of was to bring a thousand pieces of silver."

8:12: "My vineyard, which is mine, is before me, thou of Solomon, must have a thousand, and those that keep the fruit two hundred."

You are not responsible for someone else's ministry. The King is. He will only require of you what you need to keep. You will achieve more than You have ever imagined.

You can do all things!

8:13: "Thou that dwellest in the gardens, the companions hearken to thy voice…
    …cause me to hear it."

You need to hear the voice of the Holy Spirit; the voice of your *Beloved.* Talk to Him; let Him hear your voice!

He Says to Her!

8:14: "Make haste, my *Beloved,* and be!

Be thou like a roe or a young hart upon the mountains of spices!

This is what He wants you to hear!

"…as He is, so are you in this world
Believe that He has chosen you. Believe that He has prepared you. Believe that He has provided for you. Believe that all of heaven surrounds you. Believe He has opened the door for you!

Beloved, Believe! Begin!

Be!

Dear Women of God,

As beloved children of the Almighty God, we should be filled with joy and the promise of all He has for each of us. However, we are living in a day where so much of the Church, itself is wounded discouraged and without hope. The Father is raising up those He can use to bring His message of love and restoration back to the forefront. Guided by the Holy Spirit in her writings, this book proclaims the truth of that love through the beautiful pages of the Song of Solomon…..

BE-LOVED!!!!
Receive the crown, open your heart and allow Jesus Your Lord to help you dream once again.

Lori Harris
Harvest International Ministries
Texarkana, Arkansas

www.ingramcontent.com/pod-product-compliance
Lightning Source LLC
LaVergne TN
LVHW021550080426
835510LV00019B/2462